TURN

MAX LUCADO

REMEMBERING OUR FOUNDATIONS

Multnomah® Publishers *Sisters, Oregon*

TURN
published by Multnomah Publishers, Inc.
© 2005 by Max Lucado
Published in association with Anvil II Management, Ltd.

International Standard Book Number: 1-59052-450-0
Cover and interior design by studiogearbox.com
Interior typeset by Katherine Lloyd, The DESK
Cover image by Karen Beard/Getty Images

Unless otherwise indicated, Scripture quotations are from:
The Holy Bible, New International Version
© 1973, 1984 by International Bible Society,
used by permission of Zondervan Publishing House

Other Scripture quotations are from:
New American Standard Bible ™ (NASB) © 1960, 1977, 1995
by the Lockman Foundation. Used by permission.
The Living Bible (TLB)© 1971. Used by permission of
Tyndale House Publishers, Inc. All rights reserved.
The Holy Bible, New King James Version (NKJV) © 1984 by Thomas Nelson, Inc.
Holy Bible, New Living Translation (NLT) © 1996.
Used by permission of Tyndale House Publishers, Inc. All rights reserved.
The Holy Bible, New Century Version (NCV) © 1987, 1988, 1991
by Word Publishing. Used by permission.
The Message © 1993, 1994, 1995, 1996, 2000, 2001, 2002
Used by permission of NavPress Publishing Group

Multnomah is a trademark of Multnomah Publishers, Inc.,
and is registered in the U.S. Patent and Trademark Office.
The colophon is a trademark of Multnomah Publishers, Inc.
Printed in the United States of America

For information:
MULTNOMAH PUBLISHERS, INC.
POST OFFICE BOX 1720 • SISTERS, OREGON 97759
Library of Congress Cataloging-in-Publication Data
Lucado, Max.
Turn / Max Lucado.
    p. cm.
Includes bibliographical references.
ISBN 1-59052-450-0
1. Christian life. 2. Spiritual life. 3. United States--Religion. I. Title.
BV4501.3L8612 2005
243--dc22

                                                          2004027248
    05 06 07 08 09 10—10 9 8 7 6 5 4 3 2 1

To Senator John and Sandy Cornyn—
applauding your faith, vision, and leadership.

CONTENTS

"If my people, who are called by my name, will humble themselves and pray and seek my face and turn from their wicked ways, then will I hear from heaven and will forgive their sin and will heal their land."

(2 Chronicles 7:14)

INTRODUCTION

Solomon beamed. This was the greatest day of his life—arguably the greatest day in the history of Israel. The temple, the long-awaited temple, the vision of his father David, the dream of his ancestors, the temple of Israel was finally complete. The work of 70,000 laborers, 80,000 stonecutters, and 3,600 foremen finished. Pure gold covered parts of the interior. Precious inlaid stones sparkled. The ark of the covenant inhabited the Holy of Holies. From the golden altar to the woven curtains—the work was finished.

ONLY THE PRESENCE OF GOD WAS MISSING.

SO SOLOMON REQUESTED IT.

In a passionate prayer of dedication, the king cried out,

> *"Arise, O LORD God, to Your resting place,*
> *You and the ark of Your strength.*
> *Let Your priests, O LORD God, be clothed with salvation,*
> *And let Your saints rejoice in goodness."*

(2 CHRONICLES 6:41, NKJV)

The king of Israel requested the arrival of the King of the universe. And how did God respond? "When Solomon finished praying, fire came down from heaven and consumed the burnt offering and the sacrifices, and the glory of the LORD filled the temple" (2 Chronicles 7:1).

God Himself entered the temple. The people fell face-first on the pavement, declaring, "He is good; his love endures forever" (7:3). They stayed, not for one day, or two, but for *fifteen* days. They ate. They worshiped. They prayed and then, finally, "[Solomon] sent the people to their homes, joyful and glad in heart for the good things the LORD had done for David and Solomon and for his people Israel" (2 Chronicles 7:10).

Solomon retreated to his palace, probably anticipating a welcome rest.

But God had other plans.

SOLOMON WAS FINISHED WITH THE TEMPLE, BUT GOD WASN'T FINISHED WITH SOLOMON.

In the privacy of the royal chambers, God spoke again. "I have heard your prayer and have chosen this place for myself as a temple for sacrifices. When I shut up the heavens so that there is no rain, or command locusts to devour the land or send a plague among my people" (2 Chronicles 7:12–13).

Shut up the heavens? Command locusts? Why would God use

such language? Why the harsh words? Because he heard the prayer of Solomon. In his prayer of dedication Solomon had pleaded,

> *"When the heavens are shut up and there is no rain because they have sinned against You, when they pray toward this place and confess Your name, and turn from their sin because You afflict them."*

(2 CHRONICLES 6:26, NKJV)

The king understood the frailty of people's faith. And he knew God's justice does not slumber forever. God chastens His children. *And when it awakens,* Solomon in essence prayed, *and when You chasten, call us home.*

God said yes. And more than yes. He answered Solomon—and men and women down through the millennia—

in what has become one of the most beloved verses in the Bible:

> *"If my people, who are called by my name, will humble themselves and pray and seek my face and turn from their wicked ways, then will I hear from heaven and will forgive their sin and will heal their land."*

(2 CHRONICLES 7:14)

What stirs God to heal a land?

What conditions trigger refreshing rains?

What prompts the Almighty to cure a country?

The answer is the same today as it was in Solomon's time. God simply asks us to turn. He asks us...

TO TURN FROM SELF-PROMOTION TO GOD-PROMOTION ("CALLED BY MY NAME").

TO TURN FROM SELF-RELIANCE TO GOD-DEPENDENCE ("HUMBLE THEMSELVES AND PRAY").

**TO TURN FROM SELF-DIRECTION
TO GOD-DIRECTION ("SEEK MY FACE").**

**TO TURN FROM SELF-SERVICE TO REPENTANCE
("TURN FROM THEIR WICKED WAYS").**

WHEN WILL GOD HEAL THE LAND?

WHEN PEOPLE TURN BACK TO HIM.

TURN

The verb implies a decision, a redirection. I was going south, now I'll go north. Rather than drive toward a building, I'll turn and drive away from it. Turn. We understand the term. But are we willing to apply it?

More times than I care to admit, a scenario something like this has played out in our family car. Denalyn, my wife, says: "Max, you missed the turn."

My reply: "I don't think so."

"I'm looking at the map," she says.

Silence.

"Let's ask for directions," she suggests.

"Are you kidding? Did Columbus ask for directions? Did Lewis and Clark ask for directions? Do I need to ask for directions? I don't think so."

"If you don't need directions, Mr. Navigator, tell me, why are we [select the phrase according to trip]:

- in the Everglades instead of Miami?"
- headed to Knoxville rather than Atlanta?"
- seeing mountains when we should be seeing the beach?"

What response can you give to such a question?

If the terrain tells you you've made the wrong turn, it's time to make a right one. As a country, we've been traveling some rough terrain. And it's getting rougher.

In one year in America...

- Over 957, 000 marriages end in divorce.
- Over 15,000 people are murdered.
- Up to 1,800,000 pregnancies are aborted.

**DON'T WE NEED TO MAKE A TURN?
OF COURSE WE DO. BUT WHICH WAY DO WE
TURN? WHICH ROUTE DO WE FOLLOW?**

God tied His promises to Solomon (and to us) to four distinct turns:

1.TOWARD GOD'S GLORY.

2.TOWARD GOD IN PRAYER.

3. TOWARD GOD'S WORD.

4. TOWARD GOD IN REPENTANCE.

God offers to heal our land. He tells us what to do. He's done His part. Now, it's up to us.

IT'S OUR TURN.

When God says, "Heed My Word," we need to remember that He has watched countless people walk across this planet. He has watched the pain and trouble that have come from every violation of His commands. How could a loving God do less than warn us? How could He do less than set His protective fences down across the landscape of our lives and urge us to walk safely within them?

—Ron Mehl, *Right With God*, p. 58

TURN

TOWARD

GOD'S

GLORY

"If my people, who are called by my name, will humble themselves and pray and seek my face and turn from their wicked ways, then will I hear from heaven and will forgive their sin and will heal their land."

(2 Chronicles 7:14)

T U R N   # 1

A spider dropped a single strand down from the rafter of an old barn and began to weave his web. Days, weeks, and months went by, and the web grew. Its increasingly elaborate maze caught flies, mosquitoes, and other small insects, providing the spider a daily buffet of bugs.

The spider built his web larger and larger until it became the envy of all the other spiders.

One day this productive spider was traveling across his web when he noticed a single strand stretching up into the rafters.

I wonder why this is here? he thought. *It doesn't serve to catch me any dinner. It doesn't add to my pantry of insects.* Concluding that the strand was unnecessary, the spider climbed as high as he could...and severed it. In that moment, the entire web began to fall in upon itself, tumbling to the floor of the barn, taking the spider with it.[1]

Could we, as a nation, make the same mistake as that foolish spider?

Can a country spin a great web and sever it? Can she grow so successful, so smug, so self-sufficient that she forgets the strong strand that supports her? Could she look from shore to shore, survey her liberty, her strength, and her prosperity and respond, not with gratitude...but arrogance?

Recent actions make us wonder if we are doing just that.

- A verbal prayer offered in a school is unconstitutional, even if it is voluntarily participated in. If a student prays over his lunch, he must do so in silence.

- Schools resist biblical instruction. Freedom of speech is guaranteed to students, unless the topic is religious. The Ten Commandments cannot be hung on the wall of a classroom.

- God's definition of the family has come under question...even ridicule.
- A movement to remove the phrase "under God" from the Pledge of Allegiance gains disturbing momentum before being dismissed on a technicality.

A VOCAL PORTION OF THE AMERICAN POPULACE STARES AT THE STRAND OF FAITH UPON WHICH THIS COUNTRY HANGS AND ASKS:

"WHY IS THAT THERE?"

Are we forgetting the strength that holds us? We are not the first nation to suffer from amnesia. Israel was prone to forget. For that reason Moses sternly warned them:

> *"Beware that in your plenty you do not forget the LORD your God and disobey his commands, regulations, and laws. For when you have become full and prosperous and have built fine homes to live in, and when your flocks and herds have become very large and your silver and gold have multiplied along with everything else, that is the time to be careful. Do not become proud at that time and forget the LORD your God.... But I assure you of this: If you ever forget the LORD your God and follow other gods, worshiping and bowing down to them, you will certainly be destroyed."*

(DEUTERONOMY 8:11–14, 19, NLT)

National amnesia destroys nations. Forget God and pay a high price. What would our Lord have us remember? What strand would He call us to preserve? Two key ones come to mind:

America, You Exist by My Power

God determines every detail of every country. He defines all boundaries. He places every milestone. While we applaud Mayflower pilgrims and Lewis and Clark expeditions, they did nothing apart from God's power.

> *"He made from one man every nation of mankind to live on all the face of the earth, having determined their appointed times and the boundaries of their habitation."*
>
> (ACTS 17:26, NASB)

> *God Most High gave the nations their lands, dividing up the human race. He set up borders for the people.*
>
> (DEUTERONOMY 32:8, NCV)

God divides His children into people groups, separates His earth into sections, and maps out the boundaries of the nations. Summit conferences don't shape the geography of countries; God does. Leaders don't determine the future of countries; God determines the hearts of leaders.

Scripture tells us that "the king's heart is like a stream of water directed by the LORD; he turns it wherever he pleases" (Proverbs 21:1, NLT). The king may think he calls the shots, but he doesn't. God holds sway over his throne. The stubborn will of the most powerful monarch on earth is directed as easily as a farmer reroutes a shallow canal into his farm.

Remember the account of Cyrus, king of Persia? When God wanted the Jews to return to Jerusalem, He simply took over the king's heart. "God prodded Cyrus king of Persia to make an official announcement" (Ezra 1:1, *The Message*).

When Daniel needed the support of a Babylonian high official, "God [caused] the official to show favor and sympathy to Daniel" (Daniel 1:9).

When the Israelites escaped Egyptian slavery, they were poverty-stricken slaves. God not only set them free, but caused the Egyptians to equip them with supplies. God had said to Moses, "I will see to it that the Egyptians treat you well. They will load you down with gifts so you will not leave empty-handed. The Israelite women will ask for silver and gold jewelry and fine clothing from their Egyptian neighbors and their neighbors' guests. With this clothing, you will dress your sons and daughters. In this way, you will plunder the Egyptians!" (Exodus 3:21–22, NLT).

Can you imagine? This would be like post–Civil War plantation owners signing their cotton fields over to the slaves. God prompted the Egyptians to act contrary to normal human behavior.

> The LORD caused the Egyptians to look favorably on the Israelites, and they gave the Israelites whatever they asked for. So, like a victorious army, they plundered the Egyptians!
>
> (EXODUS 12:36, NLT)

God manages the hearts of all nations. For this reason David, himself a national leader, prayed: "O Lord, the God of our fathers, are You not God in the heavens? And are You not ruler over all the kingdoms of the nations? Power and might are in Your hand so that no one can stand against You" (2 Chronicles 20:6, NASB).

No wonder Paul urged: "Let every soul be subject to the governing authorities. For there is no authority except from God, and the authorities that exist are appointed by God" (Romans 13:1, NKJV).

Such words test our trust. We think of Nero, Stalin, Hitler, and Saddam Hussein. We may wonder why God permits despots and dictators their day.

BUT WE CAN BE SURE OF THIS: NO ONE RULES WITHOUT HIS PERMISSION.

HE DETERMINES NATIONAL LEADERS. AND, EQUALLY IMPORTANT, GOD DISTRIBUTES NATIONAL BLESSINGS.

Every good gift and every perfect gift is from above.

(JAMES 1:17, NKJV)

Every national privilege can be traced back to the hand of God. If we have liberty, we can thank the One who came to "proclaim liberty to the captives...to set at liberty those who are oppressed" (Luke 4:18, NKJV). If we enjoy a robust economy or a high tide of justice, we don't limit our thanks to senators or the Supreme Court; we thank God.

> **"HE MAKES NATIONS GREAT, AND DESTROYS THEM; HE ENLARGES NATIONS, AND GUIDES THEM"** (JOB 12:23, NLT).

Tally this up. God makes the boundaries. He determines the leaders. He dispenses the blessings. *And America exists by the power of God.* Can we afford to forget this—can we afford to sever this single, silver strand that supports the whole framework of our republic?

ONLY AT A TERRIBLE RISK.

> "If you ever forget the LORD your God and follow other gods, worshiping and bowing down to them, you will certainly be destroyed."
>
> (Deuteronomy 8:19, NLT)

"America," God says, "you exist by My power." That's the first reminder. But God doesn't stop there. A second reminder commands our attention.

America, You Exist for My Glory

God's name matters to God. His primary concern is His reputation. "If my people, who are *called by my name*" (2 Chronicles 7:14, italics mine). God jealousy guards His name. No one will mar or defame His glory. "Before all the people," He declares, "I will show my glory" (Leviticus 10:3, *The Message*). David reminds us that "the heavens declare the glory of God" (Psalm 19:1). God speaks of "every man, woman, and child whom I created for my glory" (Isaiah 43:7, *The Message*).

God's primary concern is not our name, but His. Not our glory, but His. Not our comfort, but His cause. God's ultimate commitment is to His reputation, not ours. Everything, including nations, exists to promote His cause.

Recall what God said through the prophet: "I will demonstrate my glory among the nations" (Ezekiel 39:21, NLT).

God does not need the United States in order to advance His cause. He lobbies no country and depends on no government. "No, for all the nations of the world are nothing in comparison with him. They are but a drop in the bucket, dust on the scales. He picks up the islands as though they had no weight at all. The nations of the world are as nothing to him. In his eyes they are less than nothing—mere emptiness and froth" (Isaiah 40:15, 17, NLT).

WE MAY THINK GOD EXISTS TO BLESS AMERICA. BUT ACCORDING TO SCRIPTURE, AMERICA EXISTS TO BLESS GOD.

Suppose—just suppose—God's glory became America's prayer and priority: "Not to us, O LORD, not to us but to your name be the glory" (Psalm 115:1). Suppose our elected officials daily asked, How can we honor God in our decisions? How can this school introduce students to God? How can this army promote the name of God?

What if America resolved to simply bless God?

"You're pipe-dreaming, Max. Why, we have legislators who disavow Scripture and mock morality. A nation that exists for the glory of God? We can't make it happen."

NO, BUT GOD CAN.

Remember, who manages the hearts of rulers? Who prompts the decisions of kings? God does. With an arch of an eyebrow He can open the coffers of Egypt, alter the policies of Babylonia, bring down a wall of communism. God can change a nation.

For that reason, we must pray—pray with all our hearts—that America would turn back to God.

> Help us, O God our Savior,
> for the glory of your name;
> deliver us and forgive our sins
> for your name's sake.

(Psalm 79:9)

Dare we apply the filter of 1 Corinthians 10:31 to our government? *"Do it all for the glory of God."* Manage budgets for the glory of God. Determine homeland security for the glory of God. Elect officials for the glory of God. Not for the glory of Democrats, Republicans, or Independents. Not for the glory of my crusade or your cause, her race or his gender, but for the glory of God.

WHEN WE PRAY SUCH A GOD-CENTERED PRAYER, GOD ANSWERS.

"If my people, who are called by my name, are sorry for what they have done, if they pray and obey me and stop their evil ways, I will hear them from heaven. I will forgive their sin, and I will heal their land" (2 Chronicles 7:14, NCV).

In 1888 (or so the legend goes), a noted chess master named Paul Morphy attended a dinner party in Richmond, Virginia. During the course of dinner, the master's attention was drawn to a painting on the wall of his host's home. The scene portrayed a young man locked in an intense chess match with the devil himself. As the artist conceived the painting, the devil's next move would claim victory— apparently entitling the evil one to the young man's soul. For this reason, the devil wore a triumphant expression, while his young opponent seemed at his wit's end.

After dinner, the famous chess champion walked over to the painting, studying the board and the pieces portrayed by the artist. After several minutes, Morphy turned to his host and declared, "I think I can take the young man's game and win!"

"Why, that's impossible!" his host replied. "Not even you, Mr. Morphy, can retrieve that game."

"Yet I think I can," the chess master answered. "Suppose

we place the men and try."

As the dinner party formed a circle around the table, the host set up the chess pieces precisely like the ones in the painting. After studying the board further, Morphy turned to the young man in the painting and smiled as if to say, "Young man, I have good news for you. He hasn't won yet. After the devil makes his move, you will get the final move."

To the surprise of everyone, Morphy bested the smug opponent in the painting. Victory was snatched from the devil and the young man was saved.

We sometimes feel like that young man in the painting. We see Satan poised to claim victory. We feel something near despair as we watch our nation make wrong turn after wrong turn, wrong move after wrong move.

But in the darkest moment God whispers,

"I HAVE GOOD NEWS FOR YOU. HE HASN'T WON YET."

GOD GETS THE FINAL MOVE. AND WE CAN URGE HIM TO TAKE IT.

WE CAN PRAY.

We must envision ourselves on a rather vicious, cosmic battlefield. Our lives are not about ourselves. This life, the "three score and ten" we live here on earth, is not about our desires and dreams, our personal fulfillment, or our happiness. Our lives are part of a much larger reality—victory over darkness both in and around us. Your life is about nothing less than the glory of God.

—Stu Weber, *Spirit Warriors*, pp. 32–33

TURN
TOWARD
GOD
in PRAYER

"If my people, who are called by my name, will humble themselves and pray and seek my face and turn from their wicked ways, then will I hear from heaven and will forgive their sin and will heal their land."

(2 Chronicles 7:14)

TURN #2

Prayer couches two surprises.

First, *God listens when we speak.* Jesus Himself assures us of that. "Ask and it will be given to you," He tells us. "If you believe, you will receive whatever you ask for in prayer" (Matthew 7:7; 21:22).

YOU MAY NOT TURN THE HEAD OF YOUR TEACHER OR KEEP THE ATTENTION OF YOUR SPOUSE. BUT WHEN YOU PRAY, GOD PAUSES.

The second surprise? *We seldom pray.* We have the greatest privilege imaginable—access to the very control center of the universe—yet rarely use it.

OUR LACK OF PRAYER SURPRISES EVEN GOD.

Through the prophet Ezekiel He lamented: "I sought for a man among them who would make a wall, and stand in the gap before Me on behalf of the land, that I should not destroy it; but I found no one" (Ezekiel 22:30, NKJV).

Upon learning that Sodom and Gomorrah were going to be destroyed, Abraham did not rush to warn the cities. He chose to "[remain] standing before the LORD" (Genesis 18:22).

When God told Moses that the golden calf warranted a nationwide death penalty for Israel, Moses interceded. One translation[2] of Exodus 32:11 says, "Moses soothed the face of Yahweh his God." (See also Exodus 32:14; Psalm 106:23.)

An obscure priest by the name of Phinehas begged God not to send a plague, and the plague was checked (Psalm 106:30).

Nehemiah learned that the city of Jerusalem had fallen into ruins.

But before he laid a foundation of stone, he laid a foundation of prayer (Nehemiah 1:4).

The apostle Paul's letters contain no appeals for money, or possessions, or comforts—but they are replete with his urgings for prayer.

But the most striking example is that of Jesus.

> *Immediately Jesus made the disciples get into the boat and go on ahead of him to the other side, while he dismissed the crowd. After he had dismissed them, he went up on a mountainside by himself to pray.*
>
> (MATTHEW 14:22–23)

If ever Jesus wanted to be king, this was the moment; this was His chance. Thrilled apostles boasted of their successful missionary journey. They had cast out demons, healed the sick, and recruited an army (Mark 6:12–13, 31). Citizens and soldiers followed them to Jesus (Mark 6:30–31). The crowd numbered five thousand men plus women and children (Matthew 14:21). *Raise the scepter Christ, and rally Your army* (John 6:15).

But He didn't.

RATHER THAN ACT, HE ASKED GOD TO ACT.

Rather than ascend the throne of power, He climbed the mountain of prayer.

> *He went up on a mountainside by himself to pray.*
>
> (MATTHEW 14:23)

Why place such a premium on prayer? Simple. When we work, we work. But when we pray, God works. Scripture attaches breathtaking power to prayer.

> *"When two of you get together on anything at all on earth and make a prayer out of it, my Father in heaven goes into action."*
>
> (MATTHEW 18:19, *The Message*)

> *We can be confident that he will listen to us whenever we ask him for anything in line with his will.*
>
> (1 JOHN 5:14, NLT)

Is any other spiritual activity promised such fruit? Did Jesus call us to preach without ceasing? Or teach without ceasing? Or have committee meetings without ceasing? Or sing without ceasing? No, but He did call us to "pray without ceasing" (1 Thessalonians 5:17, NASB).

Did Jesus say, "My house will be called a house of study"? A house of fellowship? A house of music? A house of exposition? A house of activities? A house of political activists? No, but He did say, "My house will be called a house of prayer" (Matthew 21:13).

GOD IS NOT MOVED BY MEN OF STANDING, BUT BY MEN OF KNEELING.

He is moved by the humble, prayerful heart. "The LORD will hear your crying, and he will comfort you. When he hears you, he will help you" (Isaiah 30:19, NCV).

Mark details a graphic demonstration of this truth.

> *Several days later Jesus returned to Capernaum, and the news of his arrival spread quickly through the town. Soon the house where he was staying was so packed with visitors that there wasn't room for one more person, not even outside the door. And he*

preached the word to them. Four men arrived car-
rying a paralyzed man on a mat. They couldn't get
to Jesus through the crowd, so they dug through
the clay roof above his head. Then they lowered
the sick man on his mat, right down in front of
Jesus. Seeing their faith, Jesus said to the paralyzed
man, "My son, your sins are forgiven."

(MARK 2:1–5, NLT)

You don't encounter the word *prayer* even once in that paragraph. But look closely...and you will see its portrait. Four men lowering a friend through the roof into the presence of Jesus. Christ stops preaching, looks up at the men, and then (most certainly with a twinkle) announces, "My son, your sins are forgiven."

What stirred Jesus? What prompted this surge of grace? Mark wants you to know the answer. "Seeing *their* faith, Jesus said to the paralyzed man" (v. 5, italics mine).

The faith of the friends triggered the kindness of Christ.

The paralytic in this account symbolizes all who suffer.

The man has no movement,
no treatment, no answers,
no hope. He has so little.

But what he does have is
significant: He has friends of faith.
Friends who care. Friends who help.
Friends who strategize and struggle
to present the needy to Christ.

The full house and blocked entries only doubled their resolve. "So what if the doorway is packed? We'll come at Christ from another angle." They scamper onto the roof. They scurry from one side to the next. Listeners look up. Jesus looks up. Sprinkles of dust fall from the ceiling. Chunks of roof begin to fall and the upside-down head of a friend appears. "There He is," he whispers. They yank loose more clay and start to lower their friend.

The paralytic might be gulping. ("Don't drop me!")

The homeowner might be groaning. (De-roofing is decidedly antisocial.)

But Christ? Don't you think He is smiling? Their faith stirs His strength. He heals the man. The paralytic leaves the house with a clean soul and a strong body, all because friends brought him to Christ.

FAITHFUL FRIENDS DO THIS. FAITHFUL FRIENDS CARRY STRUGGLERS INTO GOD'S SHADOW. WHEN THEY DO, HE RESPONDS.

How? When? The four men didn't know. We don't know. But we know this:

"When a believing person prays,
great things happen."

(James 5:16, NCV)

IMITATE THOSE FRIENDS, WON'T YOU?

Turn your heart to God in prayer. Carry your friends and family into the presence of God.

Lay our great nation at His feet. And take God at His word.

IF GOD'S PEOPLE DELIBERATELY, STRATEGICALLY, CEASELESSLY LIFTED THIS COUNTRY TO GOD IN PRAYER, WHAT WOULD HAPPEN?

We needn't guess at the answer. *"If my people...will humble themselves and pray...then will I hear from heaven and will forgive their sin and will heal their land"* (2 Chronicles 7:14).

Scripture insists that God has hardwired the universe in such a way that He works primarily through prayer. God has set up creation so that the way He does His work is through the prayers of His children. At the moment we pray, we become subject to the most powerful force in the universe.

—David Jeremiah, *The Prayer Matrix*, p. 4

TURN ▶

TOWARD

GOD'S

WORD

"If my people, who are called by my name, will humble themselves and pray and seek my face and turn from their wicked ways, then will I hear from heaven and will forgive their sin and will heal their land."

(2 Chronicles 7:14)

TURN # 3

The crew of the HMS *Bounty* had taken all they could take. Goaded by the cruelty of Captain Bligh, they seized control of the ship. They gave the captain and his faithfuls a boat, a push, and watched them float out to sea.

In the spring of 1789, the mutinous sailors settled on Pitcairn Island, a tiny dot in the South Pacific. The mutineers burned the ship, took Tahitian wives, and recruited Tahitian workers. It had the makings of a tropical paradise.

But they turned it into a living hell.

The sailors elevated no standard, no morals, no laws. They stirred a cesspool of adultery, violence, and drunkenness. Within a decade, the inevitable occurred. The natives attacked the settlers. Only one mutineer survived: Alexander Smith.

Left on a two-square-mile island, surrounded by natives and half-breed children, he did something remarkable. He began to read a Bible crew members had salvaged from the *Bounty*. (Today that Bible can be seen in the New York City Museum.) "When I came to the life of Jesus," Smith later explained to his superiors, "my heart began to open like doors swingin' apart. Once I was sure that God was a loving and merciful Father to them that repent, it seemed to me I could feel His very presence, sir, and I grew more sure every day of His guiding hand."[3]

Scripture transformed not just Smith, but the entire island. When the British navy discovered Pitcairn Island in 1808, its order and decency astonished them. Smith was spared, and the name *Pitcairn* became a byword for piety in the nineteenth century.

From immorality to piety. What made the difference? The Bible.

History offers a concordant chorus. Psychologist William James affirmed, "The Bible contains more true sublimity, more exquisite beauty, more morality, more important history, and finer stains of poetry and eloquence than can be collected from all other books, in whatever age or language they have been written."

Sir William Gladstone, prime minister of England, stated, "I have known ninety-five great men of the world in my time. And of these, eighty-seven were followers of the Bible."

President John Quincy Adams declared, "The Bible is the book of all others to read at all ages and in all conditions of human life."

No one remembers philosopher Immanuel Kant for orthodox religion, yet he confessed, "The existence of the Bible as a book for the people is the greatest benefit which the human race has ever experienced."

MILLIONS OF TESTIMONIES CONVERGE TO ANNOUNCE:

THE BIBLE IS THE MOST INCREDIBLE BOOK EVER WRITTEN.

What does the Bible mean to my relationship with God? It's a lot like my father's final correspondence—it gives me a glimpse of his face. I can see his letter from where I write. I keep it framed and hung in my office. When my dad was diagnosed with ALS, a disease that eventually took his life, I offered to abandon my work and move home. He penned a letter telling me not to do so. "I am not afraid of death or eternity," he wrote. "Continue your work for God."

I display the letter because it reveals the heart of my father. Want to know what kind of dad I had? Read his words.

WANT TO KNOW WHAT KIND OF FATHER WE HAVE? READ HIS WORD. GOD INVITES US TO KNOW HIM. HE DOES NOT HIDE HIS FACE; QUITE THE CONTRARY, HE UNVEILS IT.

"If you seek him, you will find him."
(1 Chronicles 28:9, NLT)

HE AWAITS OUR DISCOVERY.

"Seek the LORD while you can find him," Isaiah invites. "Call on him now while he is near" (Isaiah 55:6, NLT).

"The LORD is wonderfully good to those who wait for him and seek him" (Lamentations 3:25, NLT).

"Happy are those who...search for him with all their hearts" (Psalm 119:2, NLT).

Bottom-line these passages with one sentence:

GOD BLESSES GOD-SEEKERS.

"If you look for me in earnest, you will
find me when you seek me."

(Jeremiah 29:13, NLT)

God's face awaits our study. What makes Him smile?
What furrows His brow or sparkles His eyes? When do His
lips purse or eyes water? He wants you to know. And to
those who seek to know, He gives this promise: "If my
people...*seek my face*...then will I hear from heaven and will
forgive their sin and will heal their land" (2 Chronicles 7:14,
italics mine).

But how do we do that? How do we seek the face of an
invisible God? We read His letter. We read the Bible
because "the Scriptures point to me!" (John 5:39, NLT).
Those who want to seek His face will read His word. We can
seek His face through many venues: worship, fellowship,
meditation. But all will include the Bible.

NO OTHER BOOK COMPARES WITH IT!
CONSIDER ITS COMPOSITION.

Suppose a museum of art commissions one painting to be painted by forty different artists. They work in their respective studios, knowing nothing of each others' efforts. And yet, when these many canvases are assembled on one wall, they combine to create the perfect landscape. What are the odds?

Or consider this. Forty architects set out to design one building. Some know what others are doing—others are unaware anyone else is doing anything at all. When they gather to compile notes, the result is a magnificent blueprint. Could it happen?

It did with the Bible. No human publisher commissioned the book. No committee outlined it. No earthly editor oversaw the project. Yet, against these incredible odds, the Bible is a marvel of consistency from cover to cover. Though separated by sixteen centuries...though penned by an unlikely assortment of kings, soldiers, shepherds, farmers, and fishermen—from Moses in the lonely desert of Arabia to John on the windswept island of Patmos—one theme threads the Bible together. That theme is salvation through Jesus Christ.

James Hefley notes: "The sixty-six books are a perfect whole, a purposeful revelation and a progressive proof that the Bible is more than the work of fallible men." The Bible's composition elevates its credibility.

No wonder the Bible has endured like it has. Voltaire, the French skeptic, once wrote these words from his Paris office: "I will go through the forest of Scripture and girdle all the trees so that in one hundred years Christianity will be but a vanishing memory." Not only did he fail, but in a twist of divine irony, the very room in which he penned those words was later purchased by the British and Foreign Bible Society...and packed from floor to ceiling with Bibles.

Every passing day, every turn of the centuries validates the prophecy of Peter: "The word of the Lord will live forever" (I Peter 1:25, NLT).

What rivals the durability of the Bible? We applaud the

number one bestseller. We award the book that remains on top for weeks at a time. If one claimed the lead for several years, we would bronze each page. But what if a book is number one for *three hundred years?* The Bible makes this claim. It is the most widely published and translated book in history—available in over two thousand different dialects.

> The word of God is living and active.
> Sharper than any double-edged sword,
> it penetrates even to dividing soul and
> spirit, joints and marrow; it judges the
> thoughts and attitudes of the heart.

(Hebrews 4:12)

The Bible cuts to the heart like a scalpel. It pierces. It penetrates where the eye cannot see and touches what the hand cannot feel. Why not see for yourself?

APPLY THE BIBLE TO ANY PART OF YOUR LIFE AND SEE WHAT HAPPENS.

APPLY IT TO YOUR FINANCES. Manage your money the way the Bible says: tithe, save, provide for your family, give to the poor. Test God's Word and experience its power.

TEST GOD'S WORD ON YOUR JOB. Follow the Bible's code of work conduct. Be honest. Be on time. Be efficient. You may get a promotion.

TEST THE BIBLE ON YOUR RELATIONSHIPS. Forgive your enemies. Refuse to gossip. Do all you can to be at peace with all. Be quick to listen and slow to speak.

BUT MOST OF ALL, APPLY THE BIBLE TO YOUR SOUL. "There's nothing like the written Word of God for showing you the way to salvation through faith in Christ Jesus" (2 Timothy 3:15, *The Message*).

You want to know the real reason the Bible is incredible? Jesus is incredible. And Jesus is the main character of the Bible.

**THE BIBLE TRACES THE STORY OF THE GOD
WHO COULDN'T LEAVE US ALONE.
HE COULDN'T LEAVE US ALONE IN OUR SIN.
HE COULDN'T LEAVE US ALONE IN OUR FEAR.
HE COULDN'T LEAVE US ALONE WITH OUR DEATH.
SO GOD HIMSELF BECAME ONE OF US.
HE TOOK ON OUR FORM, OUR FLESH, AND—
MOST OF ALL—OUR SIN.**

**HE TOOK OUR PLACE SO WE COULD GO TO HIS.
THIS IS THE STORY OF THE BIBLE.
THE STORY THAT WILL CHANGE SOULS
CAN CHANGE A NATION AS WELL.**

Why would a country resist such a book? You'd think schools would *require* its study. It is, at minimum, humanity's most compelling literary work. It is, for millions, God's holy work. Does such a book not warrant sacred respect? Yet courts ban public school reading of Scripture. Judges threaten to remove the Ten Commandments from courtroom walls.

If nations exist for God's glory, how long will God bless a nation that defames His Scripture?

ON THE OTHER HAND, IF GOD'S WORD IS INDEED THE ORACLES OF HEAVEN, WHAT POWER AWAITS THE NATION THAT EMBRACES IT?

The two Emmaus-bound pilgrims can tell you. They discovered the power on the first Easter Sunday. They were brokenhearted from the Crucifixion, and "sadness was written across their faces" (Luke 24:17, NLT). Their grief blinded them to the presence of Jesus. He had risen from the dead and—though they didn't yet perceive it—He had now come to take their sorrow.

How would He do so? How would He encourage them? He owns the miracles of the universe, superintends the arsenals of the ages; the medicine chest of heaven is within His reach. What miracle, weapon, medicine will He choose? Read the answer with me:

Jesus quoted passages from the writings of Moses and all the prophets, explaining what all the Scriptures said about himself.

(LUKE 24:27, NLT)

Jesus opened their eyes, energized their heavy hearts with Scriptures. He chose the greatest miracle, weapon, and treatment of all: the Bible.

Did it make a difference? To those two men it did. "It felt like a fire burning in us when Jesus talked to us on the road and explained the Scriptures to us" (Luke 24:32).

Did it make a difference? When it came to Alexander Smith on Pitcairn Island it did. **"WHEN I CAME TO THE LIFE OF JESUS," HE SAID, "MY HEART BEGAN TO OPEN LIKE DOORS SWINGIN' APART."**

Can it make a difference in our lives? According to God it will. *"If my people... seek my face...then will I hear from heaven and will forgive their sin and will heal their land"* (2 Chronicles 7:14).

I need to be reminded of what is true.
God's Word gives me a dose of reality.
There is right and wrong; there are
consequences for making wrong choices;
the Ten Commandments are still the
standard for life; I am not to repay evil
for evil…. My morning briefing in the
Word gives a perspective that I don't get
in the world. I need God's commentary
on my life every day. A Christian…in
this society is swimming upstream.
Without the constant nutrition of the
Word, he will soon tire and be dragged
off by the sheer force of the current.

—Steve Farrar, *Point Man,* p. 111

TURN

TOWARD
GOD

IN REPENTANCE

"If my people, who are called by my name, will humble themselves and pray and seek my face and turn from their wicked ways, then will I hear from heaven and will forgive their sin and will heal their land."

(2 Chronicles 7:14)

TURN # 4

Charles Robertson should have turned himself in. That would have been his wisest move. Not that he would've been acquitted. After all, he'd just robbed a bank. He would have still gone to jail, but at least he wouldn't have been the laughingstock of Virginia Beach.

Cash-strapped Robertson, nineteen, went to Jefferson State Bank on a Wednesday afternoon, filled out a loan application, and left. He returned within a couple of hours, not to fill out another application, but to fill up a bag. He scribbled a demand on scrap paper, explaining that he had a gun and wanted money. The teller complied and all of a sudden Robertson was holding a sack of loot.

Figuring the police were fast on their way, he dashed out the front door.

He was halfway to the car when he realized he'd left the note. Fearing it could be used as evidence, he hurried back into the bank and snatched it from the teller. He scurried out the same entrance and ran a block to his parked car. That's when he realized his second mistake. He'd left his keys on the counter when he'd returned for the note.

"At this point," one detective would later chuckle, "total panic set in."

Robertson ran to a nearby fast-food restaurant and ducked into the restroom. He dislodged a ceiling tile and hid the money and the .25 caliber handgun. Scampering through alleys and creeping behind cars, he finally reached his apartment, where his roommate, who knew nothing of the robbery, greeted him with the words, "I need my car." Robertson's getaway vehicle was a loaner. Rather than confess to the crime and admit the bungle, the hapless robber dug himself deeper into the hole.

"Uh, uh, your car was stolen."

"Well, I'm calling the police!"

Robertson watched in bewildered fear while the roommate reported the stolen vehicle. About twenty minutes later an officer spotted the "stolen" car a block from the recently robbed bank. Word was already on the police radio that the robber had forgotten his keys. The officer put two and two together and tried the keys on the car. They worked.

Detectives drove to the address of the person who'd reported the stolen car. There they found Robertson. He confessed, was charged with robbery, and was put in jail. No bail. No loan. No kidding.[4]

ROBERTSON SHOULD'VE TURNED HIMSELF IN. EVERY STEP HE TOOK WAS A STEP IN THE WRONG DIRECTION. A STEP HE'D LATER REGRET.

He's not alone. Perhaps we didn't take money, but we've taken advantage or taken control or taken leave of our senses and then, like Robertson, taken off. Dashing down alleys of deceit. Hiding behind buildings of progress and success, work to be done, or deadlines to be met. We're a nation on the lam!

BUT FROM THE BEGINNING GOD HAS CALLED FOR HONESTY. HE'S NEVER DEMANDED NATIONAL PERFECTION, JUST TRUTHFULNESS.

As far back as the days of Moses, God promised: "If they will confess their sins and the sins of their fathers—their treachery against me and their hostility toward me, which made me hostile toward them so that I sent them into the land of their enemies—then...I will remember my covenant with Jacob and my covenant with Isaac and my covenant with Abraham, and I will remember the land" (Leviticus 26:40–42).

Nehemiah knew the value of honesty. Upon hearing of the crumbled walls in Jerusalem, did he fault God? Did he blame heaven? Hardly. Read his prayer:

"I confess the sins we Israelites have done against you. My father's family and I have sinned against you. We have been wicked toward you and have not obeyed the commands, rules, and laws you gave your servant Moses."

(Nehemiah 1:6–7, NCV)

The second most powerful man in the kingdom is turning himself in. Accepting responsibility for the downfall of his people. The scene of his personal confession, however, is nothing compared to the day the entire nation repented:

They stood and confessed their sins and their ancestors' sins. For a fourth of the day they stood where they were and read from the Book of Teachings of the Lord their God. For another fourth of the day they confessed their sins and worshiped the Lord their God.

(Nehemiah 9:2–3, NCV)

What a poignant picture. Hundreds of people spending hours in prayer, not making requests or excuses, but making confessions. "I'm guilty, God." "I've failed You, Father." Can you imagine members of congress and the court system spending a day in front of the Capitol offering prayers of repentance?

Consider another example. The high priest of ancient Israel places both hands on the head of the living goat. He obeys God, who instructed, "And he will confess over it all the sins and crimes of Israel. In this way Aaron will put the people's sins on the goat's head.... The goat will carry on itself all the people's sins to a lonely place in the desert. The man who leads the goat will let it loose there" (Leviticus 16:21–22, NCV).

The event gave witnesses three convictions:

GOD DESPISES SIN. GOD DEALS WITH SIN. AND OUR TASK IS TO BE HONEST ABOUT OUR SIN.

Confession does for the soul what working the acreage does for the soil. Before the farmer sows the seed he works the land, removing the rocks and pulling the stumps. Why? Seed grows better in prepared soil. God's seed grows better in a pure soul. Confession invites God to walk the acreage of our hearts. "There's a rock of greed over here, Father. I can't budge it. And that tree of racism near the fence? Its roots are long and deep. And may I show you some dry soil, too crusty for seed?"

Confession seeks pardon from God, not amnesty. Pardon accepts guilt; amnesty, derived from the same Greek word as *amnesia,* "forgets" the alleged offense without imputing guilt. Confession admits wrong and seeks forgiveness; amnesty denies wrong and claims innocence.

Peter models honest confession. Remember Peter? "Flash-the-sword-and-deny-the-Lord" Peter? The apostle who boasted one minute and bolted the next? He snoozed when he should have prayed. Denied when he should have defended. Cursed when he should have comforted. Ran when he should have stayed.

We remember Peter as the one who ran, but do we

remember Peter as the one who turned himself in? We should. Think about these questions:

How did the New Testament writers know of his sin? Who told them of his betrayal? And, more important, how did they know the details? Who told them of the girl at the gate, and the soldiers starting the fire? How did Matthew know Peter's accent made him a suspect? How did Luke learn of the glance of Jesus? Who told all four Gospel writers about the crowing rooster and flowing tears?

The Holy Spirit? I suppose. Could be that each writer learned of the moment by divine inspiration. Or, more likely, each learned of the confession by an honest confession. Peter turned himself in. Like Robertson, Peter bungled it. Unlike Robertson, Peter stopped.

HE STOPPED HIS RUNNING, FELL TO HIS KNEES, BURIED HIS FACE IN HIS FISHERMAN HANDS, AND GAVE UP.

PETER TURNED.

PETER RETURNED.

There he is, every burly bit of him filling the door frame of the upper room. "Fellows...I've got something to get off my chest." He describes that terrible morning, the fire, the girl, and the look from Jesus. They hear of the cursing mouth and the crowing rooster. He turned himself in.

How can I be so sure of this?

Peter just couldn't stay away from Christ! Who was the first to run to the empty tomb? Who was the first to jump from the boat and swim to Jesus who stood on the shore?

THOSE WHO KEEP SECRETS FROM GOD KEEP THEIR DISTANCE FROM GOD.

THOSE WHO ARE HONEST WITH GOD, HOWEVER, DRAW NEAR TO GOD.

Will America ever do this? Repent like Peter? Pray like Nehemiah and the Jews? Will this nation come clean with God? She may, if the church leads the way.

Take note of the first and final phrase of God's land-healing promise: "*If my people,* who are called by my name, will humble themselves and pray and seek my face and turn from their wicked ways, then will I hear from heaven and will forgive their sin and will *heal their land*" (2 Chronicles 7:14, italics mine).

"My people" and "heal their land." The healing of the land begins with the people of God. The nation changes when God's people change. The culture changes when the church changes. And that change begins when we repent. Genuine national repentance says: America needs to change and the change begins with me.

We don't have any problem with the first part of the sentence, "America needs to change." Our list of complaints grows like the deficit. Hollywood needs to change. Taxes need to change. The White House, the liberals, the conservatives, the lobbyists...we know what needs to change.

We begin feeling like the man at the prayer session. During the time of private prayer, he stood alone and prayed, "God, I thank You that America has people like me. The man on the corner needs welfare—I don't. The prostitute on the street has AIDS—I don't. The bum at the bar needs alcohol—I don't. The gay caucus needs morality—I don't. I thank You that America has people like me."

In the same meeting, a man of humble heart, too contrite to even look to the skies, prayed, "God, have mercy on me—a sinner. Like my brother on welfare—I'm dependent on Your grace. Like my sister with AIDS—I'm infected with mistakes. Like my friend who drinks—I need something to ease my pain. And like those You love who are gay—I need direction, too. Have mercy on me, a sinner."

After telling a story like that, Jesus said, "I tell you that this man, rather than the other, went home justified before God. For everyone who exalts himself will be humbled, but he who humbles himself will be exalted" (Luke 18:14).

ARROGANCE POINTS A FINGER AT THE PROBLEM.

HUMILITY POINTS A FINGER AT SELF AND ADMITS TO BEING A PART OF THE PROBLEM.

God's promise is clear: "If my people...will turn from their wicked ways—*if they will quit pointing at others and begin with themselves*—I will come and heal the land."

Charles Robertson didn't humble himself and confess until it was too late. He ran and ran until there was nowhere left to run. And justice had him cornered. Not so with Peter. Shocking and reprehensible as his failure and betrayal may have been, the big fisherman stopped running, turned around, and ran back toward Jesus Christ. In the presence of his Savior, Peter found the grace and mercy his heart craved, instead of the justice he deserved.

MAY IT BE SO FOR YOU AND ME.

MAY IT BE SO FOR AMERICA.

"Blessed is he whose transgressions are forgiven, whose sins are covered" (Psalm 32:1). Imagine two roads. One is clean and well traveled; the other is wretched, with deep ruts that veer off into a ditch. When a heavy snowfall blankets the two roads, both are equally covered. Just so, our sins, big and small, are equally covered by God: "Though your sins are like scarlet, they shall be white as snow; though they are red as crimson, they shall be like wool" (Isaiah 18:8).

—Erwin Lutzer, *After You've Blown It*, pp. 46–47

"If my people, who are called by my name, will humble themselves and pray and seek my face and turn from their wicked ways, then will I hear from heaven and will forgive their sin and will heal their land."

(2 Chronicles 7:14)

CONCLUSION

When our daughters were younger, we went desk hunting. I needed a new one for the office, and we'd promised Andrea and Sara desks for their rooms. Seven-year-old Sara was especially enthused. When she would come home from school, guess what she would do? Play school! I never did that as a kid. I tried to forget the classroom activities, not rehearse them. Denalyn assured me not to worry, that this is one of those attention-span differences between genders. So off to the furniture store we went.

When Denalyn buys furniture she prefers one of two extremes—so antique it's fragile or so new it's unpainted. This time we opted for the latter and entered a store of in-the-buff furniture.

Andrea and Sara succeeded quickly in making their

selections, and I set out to do the same. Somewhere in the process Sara learned we weren't taking the desks home that day, and this news disturbed her deeply. I explained that the piece had to be painted, and they would deliver the desk in about four weeks. I might as well have said four millennia.

Her eyes filled with tears. "But Daddy, I wanted to take it home today."

Much to her credit, she didn't stomp her feet and demand her way.

SHE DID, HOWEVER, SET OUT ON AN URGENT COURSE TO CHANGE HER FATHER'S MIND. EVERY TIME I TURNED A CORNER SHE WAS WAITING FOR ME.

"Daddy, don't you think we could paint it ourselves?"

"Daddy, I just want to draw some pictures on my new desk."

"Daddy, please let's take it home today."

After a bit she disappeared, only to return, arms open wide and bubbling with a discovery. "Guess what, Daddy? It'll fit in the back of the car!"

You and I know that a second-grader has no clue what will or won't fit in a vehicle, but the fact that she had measured the trunk with her arms softened my heart. The clincher, though, was the name she used: "*Daddy,* can't we please take it home?"

The Lucado family took a desk home that day.

I heard Sara's request for the same reason God hears ours. Her desire was for her own good. What dad wouldn't want his child to spend more time writing and drawing? Sara wanted what I wanted for her; she just wanted it sooner.

> When we agree with what God wants,
> He hears us as well. (See 1 John 5:14.)

Sara's request was heartfelt.

God, too, is moved by our sincerity.

The "earnest prayer of a righteous man has great power" (James 5:16, TLB).

But most of all, I was moved to respond because Sara called me "Daddy." Because she is my child, I heard her request. Because we are His children, God hears ours. The King of creation gives special heed to the voice of His family. He is not only willing to hear us, He loves to hear us. He even tells us what to ask Him: "Your kingdom come."

Your Kingdom Come

We're often content to ask for less. We enter God's presence with a satchelful of requests—promotions desired, pay raises wanted, transmission repairs needed, and tuitions due.

WE TYPICALLY SAY OUR PRAYERS AS CASUALLY AS WE'D ORDER A BURGER AT THE DRIVE-THROUGH:

"I'LL HAVE ONE SOLVED PROBLEM AND TWO BLESSINGS, CUT THE HASSLES, PLEASE."

But such complacency seems shortsighted. Here we are before the King of kings. Dare we limit our discussion? Not that our needs don't matter to Him, mind you. The pay raise is still needed and the promotion is still desired. But is that where we start?

Jesus tells how to begin. "When you pray, say: 'Father, hallowed be your name, your kingdom come'" (Luke 11:2).

When you say, "Your kingdom come," you are inviting the Messiah Himself to walk into your world. "Come, my King! Take Your throne in our land. Be present in this nation. Rule over our president. Be lord of my family, fears, and doubts." This is no feeble request. It's a bold appeal for God to occupy every corner of your life.

Who are you to ask such a thing?

You're His child, for heaven's sake!

"So let us come boldly to the very throne of God and stay there to receive his mercy and to find grace to help us in our times of need" (Hebrews 4:16, TLB).

If I, a sinful father, respond to the request of my child, how much more will our sinless God respond to us?

AVAIL YOURSELF OF THIS PRIVILEGE. SEIZE THIS OPPORTUNITY.

TURN.

TURN YOUR HEART TOWARD GOD.

WHEN YOU DO, WHEN WE DO, WHEN HIS PEOPLE DO, HE WILL HEAL OUR LAND.

By the way, the living parable of Sara and her desk didn't stop at the store. On the way home she realized that my desk was still at the store. "I guess you didn't beg, did you, Daddy?" (We have not because we ask not.)

When we unloaded her desk she invited me to christen it with her by drawing a picture. I made a sign that said

Sara's Desk. She made a sign that said I Love My Daddy. (Worship is the right response to answered prayer.)

My favorite part of the story is what happened the next day. I shared this account in my Sunday sermon. A couple from our church dropped by and picked the desk up, telling us they would paint it. When they returned it a couple of days later, it was covered with angels. And I was reminded that when we pray for God's kingdom to come, it comes!

All the hosts of heaven rush to our aid.

ACKNOWLEDGEMENTS

Many heads and hands collaborated to create this small volume. A special salute to:

—The National Day of Prayer Committee: Shirley Dobson, Vonette Bright, and Jim Wiedmann. May the words and proceeds of this project encourage your noble work.

—Steve Green, for navigating this ship through a tight fiord.

—The Multnomah Team, namely Doug Gabbert and Larry Libby. Great work!

—Karen Hill, my editorial assistant. Essential. Valuable. Wonderful.

—And my wife, Denalyn. No one loves God and country more than you. And no one loves you more than I.

N O T E S

1. Ed Young, *Been There. Done That. Now What?*
   (Nashville, TN:Broadman & Holman, 1994), 15.

2. *The Five Books of Moses,* ed. Everett Fox. *The Schocken Bible: Vol. 1*
   (New York: Schocken Books, Inc., 1983).

3. D. James Kennedy and Jerry Newcome, *What If the Bible Had
   Never Been Written?* (Nashville, TN: Thomas Nelson Publishers,
   1998), 30–31, 35.

4. Mike Mather, "Robber Leaves Keys to Getaway Car in Bank,"
   Virginia-Pilot, February 3, 1995.